NAVIGATING THE DIGITAL WILD WEST

(How to Stay Safe and Secure in an Increasingly Connected World)

(Jeffrey Friday)

COPYRIGHT AND DISCLAIMER

but not limited to special, incidental, consequential, personal, or other damages.

DISCLAIMER

The information presented here is for informational and educational purposes only. It does not construe financial or tax advice. You assume the sole responsibility of relying on this information at your own risk and we do not endorse any companies or products offered here.

TABLE OF CONTENTS

To start, you get some real-world examples of high-profile attacks. You also get a glimpse into the psyche of a cybercriminal to understand what motivates such a person, and you take a walk through the threat life cycle — from cradle to . . . well, the enterprise network.

This chapter describes the characteristics of advanced malware and botnets and dissects some of these evil critters!

CHAPTER 3: WHY TRADITIONAL SECURITY SOLUTIONS FAIL TO CONTROL APTS

Chapter 3 explains why legacy port-based firewalls, intrusion prevention systems (IPS), and other security solutions are largely ineffective in the fight against APTs.

CHAPTER 4: WHAT NEXT-GENERATION SECURITY BRINGS TO THE FIGHT.

This chapter takes a deep dive into the advanced capabilities and features of the next-generation firewall and lays out a practical methodology to protect your enterprise from APTs and cyberattacks.

CHAPTER 5: CREATING ADVANCED THREAT PROTECTION POLICIES

Chapter 5 explains the importance of developing organizational security policies and controls, and how to implement and enforce those policies with a next-generation firewall.

CHAPTER 6: TEN BEST PRACTICES FOR CONTROLLING APTS

Finally, in that classic For Dummies format, the book ends with a Part of Tens chapter chock-full of security best practices!

INTRODUCTION

We find ourselves navigating an ever-expanding digital terrain that can occasionally resemble the Wild West as our lives grow more and more electronic. We face a variety of online hazards that might jeopardize our privacy, security, and even our identities, much as explorers had to negotiate uncharted territory and contend with unforeseen dangers.

The digital world is full of potential threats, such as malware, social engineering, and cyberstalking, in addition to phishing scams and other frauds. Living in a connected world has many advantages, but there are also risks that must be understood and precautions must be taken to avoid injury.

Advanced persistent threats (APTs) have altered network and organizational security and the way that attacks are launched. These dangers and the cybercriminals behind them have never-before-seen levels of intelligence, resiliency, and patience, and are specialists at evading detection by conventional security. Multiple security disciplines must collaborate in order to control these risks. The issue of advanced threats cannot be solved by a single solution, but next-generation security offers the distinct visibility, control, and full integration of threat-prevention disciplines required to identify and counter these attacks, both known and undiscovered.

CHAPTER ONE

UNDERSTANDING THE CYBERSECURITY LANDSCAPE

The State of Today's Intrusions

Today's threats are more sophisticated and equal opportunity than ever before. All types of enterprises and information are being targeted. More and more attacks are increasingly coming to fruition, producing a steady stream of high-profile, sophisticated breaches and intrusions, including:

✓ **COMODO (BUSINESS PARTNERS).** In March 2011, an intruder compromised a reseller's network (not Comodo's own network) and stole nine digital security certificates that could then be fraudulently issued to impersonate various websites operated by Google, Microsoft, Skype, and Yahoo!, among others. This exposure illustrated the potential for attackers to gain sensitive information indirectly by attacking weak spots in a business's ecosystem.

✓ **DIGINOTAR (INTELLECTUAL PROPERTY).** In September 2011, the same attacker that claimed responsibility for the Comodo breach (see previous bullet) took credit for a much larger compromise against DigiNotar that occurred during the summer of 2011. Again, a Certificate Authority (CA) was the target and the attacker was able to generate hundreds of seemingly valid certificates for dozens of popular domains. These fraudulent certificates would enable the attacker to conduct future attacks by posing as a valid website to unsuspecting users. DigiNotar filed bankruptcy just two months after the attack was discovered. This is a profound example of how just a single attack can destroy a company's reputation and viability.

✓ **RSA (INTELLECTUAL PROPERTY).** In March 2011, RSA

Security (a division of the EMC Corporation) was infiltrated by an attacker that sent a phishing e-mail with an attached Microsoft Excel spreadsheet file to several RSA employees. The infected file contained malware that used a zeroday exploit in Adobe Flash software to install a backdoor, establish command and control, and steal passwords and sensitive data.

✓ **EPSILON (CUSTOMER INFORMATION).** In March 2011, a portion of Epsilon's (an online marketing company) clients' customer database was breached "by an unauthorized entry into Epsilon's e-mail system," exposing customer names and e-mail addresses. This information may enable an attacker to create a very credible spear phishing e-mail campaign.

✓ **SONY PLAYSTATION (CREDIT CARD DATA).** In April 2011, hackers breached the Sony PlayStation network, potentially stealing credit card and personal information (including names, birthdates, physical and e-mail addresses, passwords, logins, handles, online IDs, purchase histories, and profile data) of more than 100 million subscribers. The value of the personal information to future criminal acts — both cyber and traditional (such as kidnapping and extortion) — could easily outstrip the value of the stolen credit cards (about $1 USD each on the black market).

✓ **U.S. SENATE (POLITICAL HACKTIVISM).** In June 2011, LulzSec (a loosely organized cybercriminal group) broke into the U.S. Senate website and posted a list of compromised — but not sensitive or classified — files online. Other examples of political "hacktivism" by various criminal groups include attacks against the U.S. Public Broadcasting Service (PBS), Fox Broadcasting Company, and MasterCard, Visa, and PayPal websites in retaliation for negative coverage or adverse actions against WikiLeaks.

Spear phishing is a targeted phishing campaign that appears more credible to its victims by gathering specific information about the target, and thus has a higher probability of success. A spear phishing e-mail may spoof an organization (such as a financial institution) or individual that the recipient actually knows and does business with, and may contain very specific information (such as the recipient's first name, rather than just an e-mail address).

Spear phishing, and phishing attacks in general, are not always conducted via e-mail. A link is all that is required, such as a link on Facebook or on a message board or a shortened URL on Twitter. These methods are particularly effective in spear phishing because they allow the attacker to gather a great deal of information about the targets and then lure them into dangerous clicks in a place where the users feel comfortable.

Many organizations and individuals have been lulled into a false sense of security by the mistaken belief that the only data an attacker wants to steal — and thus the only data that needs to be protected — is financial data, such as credit card numbers or banking information. But breaches are not limited to financial data — if it's valuable to you or your organization, it's very likely to be valuable to someone else as well! As the Epsilon and Comodo examples illustrate, you don't have to have the "crown jewels" in your own network to be a victim. How secure are your partner and reseller networks?

THE CHANGING FACE OF CYBERCRIMINALS

Cybercriminals have evolved from the prototypical "whiz kid" — sequestered in a basement, motivated by notoriety, and fueled by too much carbonated caffeine — into bona fide cybercriminals, often motivated by significant financial gain and sponsored by nation-states, criminal organizations, or radical political groups. Today's attacker fits the following profile:

✓ Has far more resources available to facilitate an attack

✓ Has greater technical depth and focus

✓ Is well funded

✓ Is better organized.

Why does this matter? Because a kid in a basement may be able to break into a corporate network, but doesn't necessarily know what to do with, say, RSA source code. On the other hand, a rogue nation-state or criminal organization knows exactly what to do or who to sell stolen intellectual property to on the gray or black market.

Additionally, criminal organizations and nation-states have far greater financial resources than independent individuals.

Many criminal hacking operations have been discovered, complete with all the standard appearance of a legitimate business with offices, receptionists, and cubicles full of dutiful cybercriminals. These are criminal enterprises in the truest sense and their reach extends far beyond that of an individual.

Not only do we face more sophisticated adversaries today, but the types of information of value to them are continually expanding as well. These groups can do interesting things with the most seemingly innocuous bits of information.

The Lifecycle of an Advanced Attack

Attack strategies have also evolved. Instead of a traditional, direct attack against a high-value server or asset, today's strategy employs a patient, multi-step process that blends exploits, malware, and evasion into an ongoing coordinated network attack.

As an example, an attack often begins by simply luring an individual into clicking on an infected link. The resulting page remotely exploits the individual, gains root access on the user's computer, and downloads malware to the user's computer in the background. The malware then acts as a control point inside the network, allowing the attacker to further expand the attack by finding other assets in the internal network, escalating privileges on the infected machine, and/or creating unauthorized administrative accounts — just to name a few tactics.

The key is that instead of malware and network exploits being separate disciplines as they were in the past, they are now integrated into an ongoing process. Furthermore, malware or an exploit is not an end unto itself, but simply enables the next step of an increasingly complex attack plan. Malware, which is increasingly customized to avoid detection, provides a remote attacker with a mechanism of persistence, and the network enables the malware to adapt and react to the environment it has infected. Key components of the advanced attack strategy include infection, persistence, communication, and command and control (see Figure 1-1).

Infection

Infection often has a social aspect, such as getting users to click on a bad link in a phishing e-mail, luring them to a social networking site, or sending them to a web page with an infected image, for example. Understanding how malware and exploits have become closely interrelated in the advanced attack lifecycle is important. Exploits used to be directed at vulnerabilities on servers that were directly targeted. Most exploits today are used to crack a target system to infect it with malware: an exploit is run, causing a buffer overflow, which allows the attacker to gain shell access.

With shell access, the attacker can deliver pretty much any payload. The first step is to exploit the target, then deliver the malware in the background through the application or connection that is already open. This is known as a driveby-download and is far and away the most common delivery mechanism for advanced malware today. In fact, based on its own research, Palo Alto Networks has found that as much as 90 percent of unknown or targeted malware capable of avoiding traditional antivirus technology is delivered from real-time web applications as opposed to corporate e-mail.

Infection relies heavily on hiding from and evading traditional security solutions. Targeted attacks will often develop new and unique malware that is customized specifically for the target network. This technique allows the attacker to send in malware knowing that it is unlikely to be detected by traditional antivirus tools. Another common way to avoid security is to infect the user over a connection that security can't see into, such as an encrypted channel. Attack transmissions are often obscured in SSL-encrypted (Secure Sockets Layer) traffic or other proprietary encryption used in P2P (peer-topeer) networking applications and IM (instant messaging), for example.

Infection relies heavily on hiding from and evading traditional security solutions. Targeted attacks will often develop new and unique malware that is customized specifically for the target network. This technique allows the attacker to send in malware knowing that it is unlikely to be detected by traditional antivirus tools. Another common way to avoid security is to infect the user over a connection that security can't see into, such as an encrypted channel. Attack transmissions are often obscured in SSL-encrypted (Secure Sockets Layer) traffic or other proprietary encryption used in P2P (peer-topeer) networking applications and IM (instant messaging), for example.

The trend today is that threats do not necessarily come as an executable attachment in an e-mail. A link is all that is required. This is why social media, webmail, message boards, and microblogging platforms such as Twitter are rapidly becoming favorite infection vectors for attackers.

Persistence

Once a target machine is infected, the attacker needs to ensure persistence (the resilience or survivability of his foothold in the network). Rootkits and bootkits are commonly installed on compromised machines for this purpose. A rootkit is malware that provides privileged (root-level) access to a computer. A bootkit is a kernel-mode variant of a rootkit, commonly used to attack computers that are protected by full-disk encryption.

Backdoors enable an attacker to bypass normal authentication procedures to gain access to a compromised system. Backdoors are often installed as failover in case other malware is detected and removed from the system. Poison Ivy is one example of a backdoor that was used in the RSA attack (discussed earlier in this chapter).

Finally, anti-AV malware may be installed to disable any legitimately installed antivirus software on the compromised machine, thereby preventing automatic detection and removal of malware that is subsequently installed by the attacker. Many anti-AV programs work by infecting the Master Boot Record (MBR) of a target machine.

Communication

Communication is fundamental to a successful APT. In short, if you can't communicate, then coordinating a long-term complex attack is virtually impossible. Attackers must be able to communicate with other infected systems or controllers to enable command and control, and to extract stolen data from a target system or network.

Attack communications must be stealthy and cannot raise any suspicion on the network. Such traffic is usually obfuscated or hidden through techniques that include:

✓ **Encryption with SSL, SSH (Secure Shell), or some other custom application.** Proprietary encryption is also commonly used. For example, BitTorrent is known for its use of proprietary encryption and is a favorite attack tool — both for infection and ongoing command and control.

✓ **Circumvention via proxies, remote desktop access tools (such as LogMeIn!, RDP, and GoToMyPC),** or by tunneling applications within other (allowed) applications or protocols.

✓ **Port evasion using network anonymizers or port hopping to tunnel over open ports.** For example, botnets are notorious for sending command-and-control instructions over IRC (Internet Relay Chat) on nonstandard ports.

✓ **Fast Flux (or Dynamic DNS)** to proxy through multiple infected hosts, reroute traffic, and make it extremely difficult for forensic teams to figure out where the traffic is really going.

Command and control

Command and control rides on top of the communication platform that is established but is really about making sure that the attack is controllable, manageable, and updateable. Command and control is often accomplished through common applications including webmail, social media, P2P networks, blogs, and message boards. Command-and-control traffic doesn't stand out or raise suspicion, is often encrypted, and frequently makes use of backdoors and proxies.

THE CENTRAL ROLE OF MALWARE

Attack techniques have also evolved and malware now plays a central role in the cybercriminal's arsenal and in the lifecycle of an attack. Attackers have developed new methods for delivering malware (such as drive-by-downloads), hiding malware communications (with encryption), and avoiding traditional signature-based detection.

Unfortunately, our traditional view of malware and old security habits make us think of malware as the pea — an executable payload, perhaps attached to an e-mail. To understand, control, and successfully counter advanced threats, we need to focus on not just the pea (malware), but on all the moving parts. I explore the central role of malware in the advanced attack lifecycle further in **Chapter 2.**

KEY SECURITY LESSONS AND OPPORTUNITIES

For all their sophistication, advanced attacks exhibit some vulnerabilities of their own. Some key observations and opportunities to consider include:

✔ **Communication is the life-blood of an attack.** Today's threats are networked threats that need your network to communicate. If a threat can't communicate, the attack can be largely neutralized.

✔ **Numerous opportunities exist to detect and correlate.** By virtue of the fact that multiple steps are involved in the advanced attack lifecycle, there are multiple chances to identify and counter threats.

✔ **The framework, rather than the functionality, is the threat.** If an attacker can infect targets, persist on, communicate with, and manage infected hosts, then the attacker can do almost anything. See the threat as an extensible framework, not simply as the functionality of the specific payload.

✓ **Threats exist across multiple disciplines, so too must security.** Firewalls, intrusion prevention, antivirus, content filtering — these security solutions have traditionally been separated to provide "defense in depth." But this strategy makes it difficult — if not impossible — to identify, correlate, and counter complex, coordinated attacks that take advantage of multiple attack vectors, including

• Applications: Can hide and enable threats.

• URLs and websites: Can host and enable threats.

• Exploits: Create shell access to the target.

• Malware: controls and uses the compromised target.

• Files: Used to update malware and steal data.

✓ **Security must expand beyond the perimeter.** Organizations need to focus on expanding visibility beyond the network perimeter — both inward and outward. This is best accomplished with network segmentation and a next-generation firewall to enforce central controls on internal and external (such as remote and mobile access) network traffic.

CHAPTER TWO 2

THE ROLE OF MALWARE IN ADVANCED PERSISTENT THREATS (APTS)

In This Chapter

▸ Understanding how malware became a networked threat

▸ Examining real-world threats to the enterprise

▸ Identifying unique traits of advanced malware

INTRODUCTION

The rise of advanced malware is reshaping the threat landscape and forcing enterprises to reassess how they protect themselves. Collectively, advanced malware has outpaced traditional anti-malware strategies and in the process, has established a foothold within the enterprise that criminals and nation-states can use to steal information and attack sensitive assets. In this chapter, you learn about this new class of threat that has come to be known as advanced malware — bots, botnets, and bot-herders, what makes them tick, and what makes them particularly nasty.

Recognizing Key Characteristics of Advanced Malware

Enterprise information security teams have been doing battle with various types of malware for more than two decades. However, all of this hard-earned experience does not mean that enterprises are necessarily winning the war. Palo Alto Network's real-world analysis has consistently found that at least 40 to 50 percent of newly identified malware found in real enterprise networks lacks signature coverage from any of the top antivirus vendors. This poor "catch rate" is due to several factors. Some malware has the ability to mutate or can be updated to avoid detection by traditional malware signatures.

Additionally, advanced malware is increasingly specialized to the point where the attacker will develop a customized piece of malware that is targeted against a specific individual or network. Botnets are a particularly useful example for understanding some of the unique characteristics of advanced malware. Bots (individual infected machines) and botnets (the broader network of bots working together) are notoriously difficult for traditional antivirus/anti-malware solutions to detect. Bots leverage networks to gain power and resilience. A bot under the remote control of a human attacker (or bot-herder) can be updated — just like any other application — so that the attacker can change course and dig deeper into the network, based on what he finds or to adapt to changes and countermeasures. This is a fundamental shift compared to earlier types of malware, which were more or less a swarm of independent agents that simply infected and replicated themselves. Botnets — and a great deal of advanced malware — are centrally coordinated, networked applications in a very real sense. In much the same way that the Internet changed what was possible in personal computing, ubiquitous network access is changing what is possible in the world of malware. Now, all malware of the same type can work together toward a common goal, with each infected machine growing the power and value of the overall botnet. The botnet can evolve to pursue new goals or adapt to changes in security measures.

Distributed and fault-tolerant

Advanced malware takes full advantage of the resiliency built in to the Internet itself. A botnet can have multiple control servers distributed all over the world, with multiple fallback options. Bots can also potentially leverage other infected bots as communication channels, providing them with a near infinite number of communication paths to adapt to changing access options or update their code as needed.

Multifunctional

Updates from the command-and-control servers can also completely change the bots functionality. This multifunctional capability enables a new economic approach for a bot-herder (botnet operator), who can now use portions of the botnet for a particular task such as collecting credit card numbers, while other segments of the botnet might be sending spam. The important point is that the infection is the most important step, because the functionality can always be changed later as needed.

Persistent and intelligent

Because bots are both hard to detect and can easily change function, they are particularly well-suited for targeted and long-term intrusions into a network. Since bots are under the control of a remote human bot-herder, a botnet is more like having a cybercriminal inside your network as opposed to a malicious executable program. For example, a bot can be used to learn more about the organization of the network, find targets to exploit, and install additional backdoors into the network in case the bot is ever discovered.

Threats to the Enterprise

Given their flexibility and ability to evade defenses, botnets present an enormous threat to the enterprise. Advanced malware is virtually unlimited in terms of functionality — from sending spam to the theft of classified information and trade secrets. The ultimate impact of malware is largely left up to the attacker: a bot that was sending spam one day could be stealing credit card data the next.

Targeted intrusions

Botnets are also a key component of targeted, sophisticated, and ongoing attacks.

These types of botnets are very different than their larger brothers. Instead of attempting to infect large numbers of machines to launch malicious large-scale attacks, these smaller botnets aim to compromise specific high-value systems that can be used to further penetrate and intrude into the target network. In these cases, an infected machine can be used to gain access to protected systems and to establish a backdoor into the network in case any part of the intrusion is discovered. These types of threats are almost always undetectable by antivirus software. They represent one of the most dangerous threats to the enterprise because they specifically target the organization's most valuable information, such as research and development, intellectual property, strategic planning, financial data, and customer information.

DDoS and botnets

A slight twist on the spamming botnet model uses bots as part of a distributed denial-of-service attack (DDoS) — overwhelming a target server or network with traffic from a large number of infected endpoints. In such cases, the enterprise with the infected machine(s) is often not the target of the attack itself. Instead, the infected machine(s) is used to flood some other remote target with traffic. The bot-herder leverages the massive scale of the botnet to generate traffic that overwhelms the network and server resources of the target. DDoS attacks often target specific companies for personal or political reasons, or to extort payment from the target in return for stopping the DDoS attack. DDoS botnets represent a dual risk for the enterprise. The enterprise itself can potentially be the target of a DDoS attack, resulting in downtime and lost productivity. Even if the enterprise is not the ultimate target, any infected machines participating in the attack will consume valuable network resources and facilitate a criminal act, albeit unwittingly.

The Skunkx bot is a current example of a DDoS botnet. It is capable of performing a variety of DDoS attacks including UDP floods, SYN floods, and HTTP floods and is commonly spread over MSN and Yahoo! Messenger.

Botnets: Attack or Defend?

The explosion of botnets has certainly not gone unnoticed in the security industry. Many organizations have teamed up with law enforcement to take action against some of the largest and most notorious botnets. The goal is to separate the bots (the infected machines) from their brain (the command and-control servers). If the bots can't get to their servers, they can't get new instructions, upload data, or do any of the things that make botnets so dangerous (see Figure 2-2). This "attack" or "top-down" approach is often referred to as a botnet "decapitation" or "takedown." While these takedown efforts are important, they are not practical undertakings for most organizations and should not be confused with or distract security teams from actually protecting an enterprise from advanced malware. The most obvious limitation to this "top-down" approach is that it is incredibly time and resource intensive, and as such, only the largest and most notorious botnets are targeted. As discussed earlier in this chapter, some of the most dangerous types of malware are those used in targeted intrusions, and thus they are not particularly large and are not likely to get widespread attention.

Finally, successfully decapitating or taking down a botnet can take several years. Enterprise security needs are far more immediate — ensuring that an intrusion or exploit does not succeed in the first place (see Figure 2-3). In a very real sense, relying on the security industry to disable a botnet is like waiting for the government to enact a law against an act that someone is committing against you right now.

So while progress has been made attacking botnets at a global level, the simple truth is that the wins provide little solace to an enterprise that is under attack today. This puts the responsibility for protecting the enterprise from botnets squarely on the shoulders of the enterprise itself. In Chapter 3, I discuss what doesn't work, and then in Chapter 4, I tell you what does work in the fight against advanced malware!

Enterprise security teams rarely need to take down an entire botnet at the source. Instead, your security team needs to be more narrowly focused on such things as preventing infections, finding machines that are infected, and limiting the scope of any damage. In short, your goal is not to be Eliot Ness aiming to take down Al Capone, but to be the local beat cop — keeping your community safe from Al Capone's criminal activities.

Analyzing the Indestructible Botnet: TDL-4

In mid-2011, security researchers began tracking a new version of the TDL botnet, which is alternately known as TDSS or Alureon. This new variant — TDL-4 — has built-in mechanisms that protect the botnet from a traditional decapitation takedown, such as Microsoft's takedown against the Rustock botnet in early 2011. These "features" have led some in the security industry to label TDL-4 as "indestructible." In TDL-4, as with most advanced malware, the threat is more about the framework than the actual payload or application. TDL-4 is primarily spread through affiliates — often pornographic, piracy (software, movie, and music), and video/file sharing websites — that are paid as much as $200 USD for every 1,000 computers that they infect (see Figure 2-4).

Persistence is achieved through installation of a bootkit that infects the Master Boot Record (MBR) of the victim machine, and more than 20 additional malware programs, including fake antivirus programs, adware, and a spamming bot. Very cleverly, TDL-4 actually removes approximately 20 common malware programs — such as Gbot and ZeuS — to avoid drawing unwanted attention to a victim computer when legitimately installed antivirus software detects these common malware programs on the computer! Communications are concealed using proprietary encryption that is tunneled within SSL. TDL-4 can also install a proxy server on an infected machine, which can then be rented out as an anonymous browsing service that proxies traffic through numerous infected machines. That's right! You're familiar with Software as a Service (SaaS), Infrastructure as a Service (IaaS), and Platform as a Service (PaaS) — get ready for Malware as a

Service (MaaS)! For command and control, TDL-4 uses the Kad P2P network, a publicly accessible P2P file exchange network. TDL-4 updates and distributes information about infected machines over the Kad network, so that even if a command-and-control server is taken down, other infected bots can be found to maintain the botnet — without command-and-control servers. While all that certainly sounds ominous, there is an important distinction between the way that the security industry goes about completely dismantling a botnet and the steps that an enterprise should undertake to protect itself from that same botnet. A whole host of challenges make botnet takedowns very challenging, not the least of which is the need to take down the entire command-and-control infrastructure in a relatively short window of time. I cover this and other botnet security challenges in the next section. Advanced malware depends on the enterprise network in order to survive. In the truest sense, advanced malware consists of networked applications that are uniquely designed to evade traditional security solutions. To detect and stop these threats, security teams need to regain full visibility into network traffic, reduce the exposure of the network and user, and establish new techniques to detect and prevent advanced malware. These techniques exist today and are discussed in Chapter 4.

CHAPTER THREE 3

WHY TRADITIONAL SECURITY SOLUTIONS FAIL TO CONTROL APTS

In This Chapter

▶ Recognizing the limitations of legacy security controls

▶ Exploring the hidden nature of advanced malware

▶ Looking at signature-based detection

▶ Turning to targeted malware

▶ Understanding the need for a fully integrated security solution

The Rapidly Expanding Attack Surface

In the past, exploits targeted servers and malware was delivered to end-users through e-mail. These threats were largely independent and were handled in different ways. Today, exploits also target end-users and work hand in glove with a number of applications to deliver malware to users in unexpected ways. The applications include:

✓ File transfer apps

✓ Instant messaging

✓ Webmail

✓ Social media platforms

✓ Microblogging

✓ Workflow and collaboration applications

This means that attackers have far more targets for their attacks and an expansive arsenal of tools to use against those targets. To make matters worse, these applications often operate on a real-time model. Hardly anyone notices e-mail delays as messages are inspected for malware on an e-mail server prior to delivery. But now threats are streamed using browsers and any number of other application platforms that, if delayed, will elicit widespread complaints from users.

A Lack of Visibility

In order to maximize their accessibility and use, many applications are designed from the outset to circumvent traditional port-based firewalls by dynamically adjusting how they communicate — often bringing malware along for the ride. APTs have taken this trend and expanded upon it considerably. Simply stated, you can't control threats that you can't see, and APTs use a variety of tricks to hide their true nature or existence on the network, including:

✓ **Nonstandard ports and port hopping.** Evasive applications are one of the key factors leading to the demise of traditional port-based firewalls. However, traditional IPS and threat products also rely heavily on port to determine which signatures or analysis to apply to the traffic. This weakness is magnified by the fact that APTs are often communicated from the inside of an infected network back to the remote attacker outside. This gives the attacker full flexibility to use any port, protocol, and encryption that he wants — fully subverting any portbased controls in the process.

✓ **SSL encryption.** Malware creators rely heavily on various forms of encryption to hide the infection of traffic, as well as the ongoing command-and-control traffic associated with botnets. SSL is a favorite, simply because it has become a default protocol for so many social media sites, such as Gmail and Facebook. These sites are coincidentally very fertile ground for social engineering and malware delivery. As a result of SSL encryption, many IT security teams lack the ability to see malware traffic on their network. Other types of encryption have also become popular for hiding malware traffic. Peer-to-peer applications provide both infection and commandandcontrol capabilities, and often use proprietary encryption, again allowing malicious content to pass through the traditional network perimeter undetected.

✓ **Tunneling.** Tunneling provides yet another tool for attackers to hide malicious traffic. Many applications and protocols support the ability to tunnel other applications and protocols within them. This lets attackers disguise their communications as allowed services or applications to get past traditional perimeter security solutions.

✓ **Proxies.** Advanced malware and hackers use proxies to traverse traditional firewalls. TDL-4, the "indestructible botnet" (refer to Chapter 2) installs a proxy server on every host that it infects. This allows the bot to not only protect its own communications, but also to establish an anonymous network that anyone can use to hide his tracks while hacking or conducting other illegal activities.

Anonymizers and circumventors. Tools such as UltraSurf, Tor, and Hamachi are purpose-built to avoid network security controls. Unlike most of the other technologies discussed in this section, circumventors have almost no legitimate use in an enterprise network. These applications are updated on a monthly (and even weekly) basis to avoid detection in a perpetual cat-and-mouse game with traditional security solutions.

✓ **Encoding and obfuscation.** Malware almost always encodes transmissions in unique ways. Encoding and obfuscation not only help them avoid detection signatures, but also hide the true goal of the malware. This technique can be as simple as converting strings to hexadecimal, or as sophisticated as developing custom algorithms for detailed translations.

Signature Avoidance

The traditional approach to detecting and blocking malware is based on the simple notion of collecting samples of malware and then writing a signature for that sample. Even at its best, this approach has several drawbacks simply due to the reactive nature of the strategy. By design, protection can't be delivered until the malware is already "in the wild," during which time networks are blind to the threat. In order to provide protection for enterprise networks, a sample of new or unknown suspicious traffic must be captured and identified before a detection signature can be created by security vendors. This means that some users and networks will be successfully breached by new malware until a new detection signature is created and downloaded. This reactive model creates a window of opportunity for attackers, leaving enterprise networks vulnerable — sometimes for weeks or even months — until new malware is suspected, collected, analyzed, and identified. During this time, attackers have free reign to infect networks and users. Advanced malware has taken this weakness and expanded upon it by evolving techniques to avoid being captured in the wild and to avoid the signatures that have already been created. Targeted malware and polymorphism, discussed in the next sections, are increasingly common techniques used to exploit the inherent weaknesses of signature-based detection.

Polymorphism

Polymorphism has been used by malware for some time, but continues to be popular today. This approach aims to avoid signatures by regularly mutating to avoid simple signature matches. Some malware applications have entire sections of code that serve no purpose other than to change the signature of the malware.

Traditional Network Controls Are Ineffective

Traditional network security solutions simply were never designed to meet the challenges of advanced malware. Traditional firewalls and IPS solutions classify traffic, a firewall allows or blocks traffic, and an IPS determines which signatures to apply, all based on port. As a result, a threat that is evasive and dynamic, such as advanced malware, can simply bounce to an unexpected port, gain access to the network, and avoid detection.

Firewalls

Port-based firewalls are often used as a first line of defense, providing coarse filtering of traffic and segmenting the network into different password-protected zones. One drawback to port-based firewalls is that they use protocol and port to identify and control what gets in and out of the network. This port-centric design is ineffective when faced with malware and evasive applications that hop from port to port until they find an open connection to the network. Such firewalls themselves have little ability to identify and control malware. Solutions that have added anti-malware capabilities to portbased firewalls either as a blade module or as a UTM (Unified Threat Management) platform have typically suffered from poor accuracy and severe performance degradation.

Intrusion prevention

IPSs provide a step in the right direction, in that they look much deeper into the traffic than a firewall does. However, IPS solutions typically don't run a complete set of IPS signatures against all traffic. Rather, the IPS attempts to apply the appropriate signatures to specific types of traffic, based on port. This limitation means that malware or exploits on unexpected or nonstandard ports are likely to be missed. Additionally, IPS solutions lack the depth of malware detection needed to protect networks — most IPS solutions only look for a few hundred types of common malware — well short of the tens of thousands that exist.

Proxies

Proxy solutions are another means of network traffic control. But they too look at a limited set of applications or protocols and only see a partial set of the network traffic that needs to be monitored. By design, proxies need to mimic the applications they are trying to control so they struggle with updates to existing applications and new applications. As a result, although proxies understand a few protocols in depth, they typically lack the breadth of protocol support needed to control the tunnels and protocols within protocols that hackers use to hide their true traffic. A final issue that plagues proxy solutions is throughput performance, caused by the manner in which a proxy terminates an application on the proxy and then forwards it on to its destination. The challenge with any of these network controls is that they do not have the ability to accurately identify applications and malware; they look at only a portion of the traffic and suffer from performance issues. Security policies must be based on the identity of users and the applications in use — not just on IP addresses, ports, and protocols. Without knowing and controlling exactly who (users) and what (applications and content) have access to the network, enterprise networks may be compromised by applications and malware that can easily bypass port-based network controls.

Crossing Legacy Security Silos

Over the years, enterprises have tried to compensate for the inherent deficiencies in port-based firewalls by implementing a range of supplementary security devices, such as host-based solutions and standalone appliances. IDS and Firewall.

Network versus host-based approaches

Traditionally, enterprises have focused most of their antimalware time and resources at the end-users' desktops, typically in the form of host antivirus, personal firewalls, and the like. However, as malware evolves from individually infected endpoints to coordinated malware networks, enterprises need to expand their security perspective to incorporate networklevel intelligence and controls to complement end-point security measures. Network security has the unique advantage of allowing you to focus on the very trait that distinguishes botnets from earlier forms of malware — its reliance on communication with a larger bot network. To twist John Gage's famous phrase, "the network is the computer," in a very realsense the threat itself has become a network. If your security measures don't operate at this same level, you run a very real risk of missing the forest for the trees.

Additionally, network security mechanisms provide an independent layer of monitoring and control, unlike the endpoints themselves, which can be compromised by malware. Botnets and advanced malware can include rootkits that gain rootlevel access to subvert antivirus protections or other security mechanisms on the target machine. This creates a paradox for the security team, since any security software running on a compromised host cannot truly be trusted. This certainly doesn't imply that host-based security is obsolete, but rather illustrates that blended threats against both the host and the network will likewise demand a security response that leverages the unique strengths of both the host and network security measures.

Integrating multi-disciplinary solutions

Stopping APTs and cyberattacks requires an integrated, multidisciplinary approach to detect malicious traffic, correlate events, and respond accordingly in the enterprise network. Many organizations have deployed various security solutions in addition to their legacy port-based firewalls, including intrusion prevention systems (IPS), proxy servers, webcontent filtering, antivirus gateways, and application-specific solutions — such as instant messaging or e-mail security (anti-spam) appliances — in an effort to shore up their defenses against advanced malware threats. However, this cobbled-together approach to security infrastructure creates problems of its own, such as:

✓ Not everything that should be inspected actually is, because these solutions either can't see all of the traffic or rely on the same port- and protocol-based classification scheme as port-based firewalls.

✓ Information is not easily correlated, and the all-important context between events is lost due to security solutions being separated into their specialized silos.

✓ Policy management, access control rules, and inspection requirements are spread across multiple devices and consoles, making it difficult to develop and enforce a consistent enterprise security policy.

✓ Performance suffers due to relatively high aggregate latency because the same traffic is scanned and analyzed on multiple devices.

More security appliances don't necessarily mean a more secure environment. In fact, the complexity and inconsistency associated with such an approach can actually be a detriment to your organization's security. How? By overwhelming your security team with data from multiple sources that cannot be easily correlated and analyzed.

CHAPTER FOUR 4

WHAT NEXT-GENERATION SECURITY BRINGS TO THE FIGHT

In This Chapter

▶ Addressing legacy blind spots with a next-generation firewall

▶ Keeping the enterprise safe from malware infections

▶ Finding the indicators of compromise already in the network

The next-generation firewall provides arguably the most important weapon in the fight against advanced malware — the reliable visibility and control of all traffic on the network, irrespective of port or evasive tactics that may be employed. Put simply, if you don't fully analyze all traffic, you can't protect yourself from the threats it carries. In this chapter, I propose a methodology to limit exposure to malware — as well as to detect and remediate network devices that may already be infected — using the visibility and control capabilities of the next-generation firewall.

INTRODUCING THE NEXT GENERATION FIREWALL

By understanding the full stack behavior of all traffic on the network, you can finely control the behaviors that are allowed in the corporate environment and eliminate the shadows that APTs use to hide. These attacks quite simply must talk in order to function. Finding these telltale communications is a critical component of controlling cyberattacks and the threats they pose.

A next-generation firewall performs a true classification of traffic based not simply on port and protocol, but on an ongoing process of application analysis, decryption, decoding, and heuristics. These capabilities progressively peel back the layers of a traffic stream to determine its true identity (see Figure 4-1). The ability to pinpoint and analyze even unknown traffic — without regard to port or encryption — is the defining characteristic of a true next-generation firewall and is invaluable in the fight against APTs. Cybercriminals thrive on their ability to blend in with approved or "normal" traffic. The quality of your visibility into that traffic is one of your most critical assets. Additionally, the next-generation firewall provides a fully integrated approach to threat prevention in a unified context: true coordination of multiple security disciplines (for example, application identity, malware and exploit detection, intrusion prevention, URL filtering, file type controls, and content inspection), as opposed to simply co-locating them on the same box. This integration provides a far more intelligent and definitive understanding of malware than any individual technology can provide by itself — and is needed in order to see and understand the telltale signs of unknown threats.

PREVENTING INFECTION WITH NEXT-GENERATION FIREWALLS

One of the most important steps that an enterprise can take to control advanced malware is to reduce attack vectors and eliminate the ability for bots to hide in the network. Today the majority of vectors used by malware is virtually unchecked, and malware traffic is typically small enough to easily blend into the background of "normal" network traffic. By regaining full visibility and control of exactly what traffic is allowed into the network and why, security teams can accomplish both of these goals.

Reduce the attack surface

Enforcing positive control is essential to the fight against malware. Positive control greatly reduces the attack surface and mitigates overall risk. Thus, an important first step for the enterprise is to return to a positive control model. Positive control simply means allowing only the specific applications and traffic you want, instead of trying to block everything that you don't want. Positive control has long been a defining characteristic of network firewalls that separates them from other types of network security devices. For example, if you want to permit Telnet, you allow TCP port 23 through your firewall. Unfortunately, traditional firewalls cannot properly delineate other applications and protocols that may also be using port 23. Applications and malware now use non-standard, commonly open ports (for example, TCP port 80, 443, and 53) or simply hop between any available open ports to evade traditional firewalls. Extending positive control to include all applications, irrespective of port, is not as easy as simply flipping a switch. Employees may use certain applications that do not have a readily apparent business value. Additionally, some applications may be used for both personal and business purposes. For example, Facebook can be used for social networking buthas also become an increasingly important tool for many company marketing, sales, and recruiting initiatives. As such, organizational IT security teams should consult appropriate groups and departments within the organization to determine approved applications and uses and to establish appropriate policies. These policies should allow only certain users to access specific applications, or limit the use of specific applications to certain approved features.

To reduce the attack surface, enterprises must

✓ Enforce positive control of all network traffic to prevent unnecessary or high-risk traffic, even when encryption or port evasion techniques are used to hide the traffic.

✓ Establish policies for approved applications and uses based on business needs and culture, by determining

• What applications and protocols are in use on the network?

• What applications are required for the business and who needs to use them?

• What dual-use or personal applications does the enterprise want to allow?

Control advanced malware enabling applications

Applications are an indispensible part of the attack lifecycle, and are critical to both the initial infection of the target machine and the ongoing command and control of the attack. The association between malware and applications is not new. In the past, the de facto enabling application for malware was corporate e-mail. From a security perspective, viruses and e-mail simply went hand-in-hand. Although e-mail is still used by attackers, it has lost some of its luster as e-mail security has become a focal point for many enterprises. Attackers have shifted much of their attention to softer target applications that interact with users in real-time and provide far more threat opportunities. Attackers have gravitated to applications that facilitate social engineering while hiding the presence of compromise. Social networking and personal use applications meet both of these criteria, and are among the most common sources for malware infection and subsequent command and control (see Figure 4-2). These applications include social networking, web-based e-mail, instant message (IM), peer-to-peer (P2), and file transfer.

These applications are designed to easily share information in a variety of ways, and people often use them with an implied trust and a more cavalier attitude because they may be accustomed to using them outside of the office. This provides an attacker with a multitude of infection opportunities. Social applications also present an ideal environment for social engineering, enabling an attacker to impersonate a friend or colleague, for example, to lure an unsuspecting victim into clicking a dangerous web link. For all their sophistication, malware infections continue to rely on enticing an unsuspecting user into performing an ill-advised action, such as clicking a malicious link. Instead of opening an e-mail attachment, the click may be a link in a tweet or on a Facebook Page that appears to be from a friend. Cross-site scripting can populate dangerous links among friends, and packet sniffing technologies such as FireSheep allow attackers to take over social networking accounts. These materials are:

Control SSL in context

Social networking sites are inadvertently making it easier for malware to remain hidden by moving to the default use of SSL to protect user communications. Twitter has recently joined the ranks of fellow social media giants Facebook and Google by moving to more widespread and default use of SSL to protect their end-users' information. Twitter recently announced that users can set a preference to secure all Twitter communication via HTTPS, which will in time become the default setting for the Twitter service. This shift to default SSL encryption highlights a very real and important challenge for enterprise security that boils down to this:

✓ Social media applications continue to be the preferred point of infection between enterprise networks and targeted attacks.

✓ Organizations that lack the ability to dynamically look within or enforce security on SSLencrypted communications are more or less blind to this potentially malicious traffic.

The ramifications for enterprise security are clear: If you can't control social media — and specifically social media that is SSL-encrypted, then you are leaving a clear path open for malware to get into and out of your network. The shift to SSL by default provides a moderate improvement in privacy for the users, but in the process makes the enterprise far more vulnerable to organized attacks, lost data, and compromised systems.

Actively test unknown files

Malware and exploits are easily modified or customized by attackers so that their attack will not trigger known signatures. This flexibility is one of the key technologies that allows an advanced attacker to gain a foothold within a target network without arousing the suspicion of security. To address this shift by attackers, you need to integrate new technologies that can identify unknown threats based on how it behaves, not simply based on how it looks. This sort of active analysis can be performed by executing suspicious files in a virtual sandbox. A sandbox is a fully virtualized environment where you can run and observe a suspect file to see what the file really does, providing a way of detecting new threats.

However, detection is only part of the battle. Enforcement against these threats is still needed in order to keep the network and its users safe. This makes it critical for the active analysis malware to be tightly linked with the next-generation firewall so that results of the analysis can be used for enforcement. Typically in-line enforcements include

✓ Dynamic protections for newly identified unknown malware, zero-day exploits, and their variants.

✓ Protections for related malware that may use the command and control servers or infrastructure

✓ Protections for threats that leverage the same command and control strategy

✓ Protections for threats that use related domains and URLs Control enabling applications by:

✓ Blocking the use of known "bad" applications, such as P2P file-sharing

✓ Limiting application usage to users and groups that have a legitimate and approved business need

✓ Disabling specific features in risky applications, such as file transfers, desktop sharing, and tunneling

✓ Preventing drive-by-downloads from compromised web pages that automatically download malicious files without the user's knowledge

✓ Decrypting SSL traffic selectively, based on application and URL categories (for example, decrypt social networking and webmail, but not financial traffic)

✓ Inspecting and enforcing any risky application traffic that is permitted using a next-generation firewall that provides truly integrated intrusion and threat prevention, malware protection, and URL filtering

Prevent use of circumventors

Common end-user and Web 2.0 applications can be co-opted by malware for use against the enterprise. Equally important,

Another class of applications are proactively designed to evade traditional network security. These applications include

✓ Remote desktop technologies

✓ Proxies

✓ Purpose-built circumventing applications

Some of these applications have valid business uses, while others are a sure sign of unauthorized and dangerous behavior. In all cases, they require tight control to prevent unmanaged threat vectors into the enterprise. Remote desktop technologies are popular among end-users and IT support teams. Many web-conferencing applications have added the ability to remotely control a user's machine. Such technologies introduce two important risks: ✓ When a user connects to a remote PC, he is free to surf to any destination and use any application without that traffic being inspected by the firewall. In addition to circumventing policy, the remote desktop opens an unmanaged threat vector by allowing a user to remotely undertake all kinds of risky behavior and then have the results tunneled back to his machine inside the enterprise.

✓ Remote desktop technologies potentially allow an unauthorized user to gain full access to a machine inside the trusted enterprise network. This type of remote control is one of the first objectives of malware, and as such it creates a dangerous opportunity to launch an intrusion. According to Verizon's 2011 Data Breach Investigations Report, 71 percent of breaches and 27 percent of records lost can be attributed to remote access.

Common applications that have valid uses within the enterprise can also create unintentional exposures if improperly used, or used by unauthorized or untrained users. For example, many IT departments use SSH to manage systems and applications in a corporate datacenter. By opening a tunnel into the datacenter, SSH can provide direct, unmanaged access into an enterprise's most critical assets. These applications need to be tightly controlled, limited to approved individuals only, and closely monitored and logged.

Finally, a variety of web proxies and encrypted tunneling applications have been developed to provide secure and anonymous communication across firewalls and other security infrastructure. Proxy technologies such as CGIProxy or PHProxy provide a relatively easy way for users to surf securely without enterprise control and have been found in more than 75 percent of enterprise networks. Applications such as UltraSurf, Hamachi, and Tor are purpose-built to traverse security infrastructures and are regularly updated in order to remain undetected. These applications have very few, if any, valid uses within the enterprise, and their presence generally indicates an attempt to avoid enterprise security. These tools not only pass traffic without being inspected, but they also tend to be used for high-risk behaviors, such as file sharing or accessing expressly blocked content and sites that, in turn, carry a significantly higher risk of malware infection. These applications should be blocked in almost all cases. Prevent the use of circumventors by:

✓ Limiting remote desktop use, for example, to IT support personnel only

✓ Securely enabling SSH but preventing SSH tunneling

✓ Blocking unapproved proxies and encrypted tunnels, such as UltraSurf and Hamachi

Investigate any unknown traffic

Once an enterprise has regained positive control and has the ability to inspect and accurately classify approved traffic on its network, it can examine any remaining unknown traffic on the network. Malware and APT traffic often appear as "unknown" due to their unique behavior and use of proprietary encryption. Unlike traditional firewalls that typically pass any traffic that uses an approved port, a next-generation firewall provides the ability to find and analyze unknown traffic in the network. Unknown traffic regularly sent by the same client machine should be investigated to determine whether it is beinggenerated by a legitimate application that is not recognized or by a potential malware infection. Security teams can also investigate where the traffic is going:

✓ Does it go out to known malicious websites or to social networking sites?

✓ Does it transmit on a regular schedule?

✓ Does someone attempt to download or upload files to an unknown URL?

Any of these behaviors can indicate the presence of a bot on the client machine. Using a next-generation firewall to accurately identify traffic on the network, "unknown" traffic should become increasingly rare, thus enabling potentially malicious traffic to be quickly found and analyzed. Increasingly, the next-generation firewall goes beyond analyzing unknown traffic and can even automatically analyze unknown files in a sandbox environment to identify the malicious behaviors of threats. This allows you to focus on unknown files and unknown traffic. Unknowns on the network need to be investigated, identified, and managed. You can quickly and systematically manage unknown traffic by:

✓ Applying a policy on the firewall to block all unknown traffic, or allow and inspect it.

✓ Determining what internal applications exist on the network, and either applying an application override (renaming the traffic) or creating a custom signature.

✓ Analyze unknown or suspicious files in a sandbox to uncover malicious behaviors.

✓ Using packet captures (PCAP) to record the unknown traffic and submit it to your security vendor.

✓ Utilizing behavioral botnet reports and other forensics or reporting tools to determine whether the traffic is a threat.

Investigate "unknown" traffic for potential unauthorized user behavior or malware activity:

✓ Track source, destination, and volumes of unknown traffic

✓ Correlate against URL, IPS, malware, and file-transfer records

✓ Define custom application IDs for any internal or custom applications, as needed

✓ Deliver packet captures (PCAPs) to your security vendor for further analysis and identification

Finding Infected Hosts with Next-Generation Firewalls

Even with the best of controls, enterprise machines will inevitably be infected with malware — perhaps through a new type of malware, an unknown vector, or a USB drive. Malware has proven time and again that it is possible to infect even the most heavily secured systems. Thus, it is prudent to assume endpoints are infected and develop the skills necessary to find infected endpoints in the network. This can be a challenging task, given that a bot may have already avoided traditional malware signatures and may already have root-level access on an infected machine. To pinpoint infected machines, your focus must shift from malware signatures. Instead, you need to analyze unusual or unknown behaviors that are observed on the network. Communication is the Achilles' heel of advanced malware. It must communicate in order to function and must be difficult to find and trace. These basic requirements create patterns that can be used to identify bot traffic or behaviors that stand out from the normal network traffic — even if the bot is completely new and unknown.

Find command-and-control traffic

One of the major advantages of a next-generation firewall is its ability to classify potentially complex streams of traffic at the application level. This includes the ability to progressively scan within traffic and peel back protocols running within protocols, until the true underlying application is identified. The ability to identify complex traffic is crucial to detecting the unique command-and-control traffic of advanced attacks. For all intents and purposes, a botnet is an application and its unique traffic can be identified by a true next-generation firewall.

Automate tracking and correlation

The techniques described in the previous sections are crucial, but many organizations don't have the time for manual investigations. A next-generation firewall can automate tracking and correlation with intelligent capabilities including

✓ **Unknown TCP/UDP.** APT traffic is often encrypted and unknown. Tracking unknown TCP and UDP activity is a great starting point for finding bot-infected machines.

✓ **Dynamic DNS (DDNS).** Malware will often use DDNS to bounce traffic between multiple infected hosts with an ever-changing list of IP addresses, making it very difficult to track the true source and destination of a bot.

✓ **Known malware sites.** The URL filtering engine of a next-generation firewall constantly tracks sites that have hosted malware whether intentionally or unintentionally.

✓ **Recently registered domains.** Malware often uses new domains as it moves around to avoid detection and to recover. Repeated visits to a newly registered domain are not conclusive, but may be evidence of an infection.

✓ **IP addresses instead of domain names.** Bots often use IP addresses, as opposed to normal user (human) browsing that typically prefers friendly URL addresses.

✓ **IRC traffic.** IRC traffic is one of the most well-known communication methods for botnets, and provides additional evidence of a bot infection.

CHAPTER FIVE 5

CREATING ADVANCED THREAT PROTECTION POLICIES

In This Chapter

▶ Developing effective governance

▶ Applying policies and controls to protect mobile users and devices

Far too often, technical solutions are implemented without considering the implications for an organization's overall security strategy. To avoid this mistake, it is important to ensure that your policies are up to date and the technology solutions you are considering support a comprehensive security strategy. This chapter describes the different types of controls that must be considered in an organization's security policies.

SAFE ENABLEMENT THROUGH SMART POLICIES

The purpose of enterprise security policies is to reduce the risk of being infected by advanced threats in the first place. But, as discussed in Chapter 1, even the most secure networks with the best security policies are inevitably susceptible to malware and attacks. Likewise, you have to assume that your network will eventually be breached, no matter how well designed your policies are, and plan accordingly. Chapters 3 and 4 cover techniques for detecting and stopping breaches.

Your security policy must help your organization control malware and reduce risks, while also meeting your business requirements. Creating effective security policies requires a keen understanding of the risks posed by the various applications and features used in your network, the business needs of the organization, and your users' work requirements. IT must play an active role in defining smart policies that enable an organization's users and mitigate risk, but it is important for IT not to be the sole owner of these policies — visible executive support is critical. Adoption of new applications in organizations tends to start from the users themselves, not from policies. But once these applications become integrated into business processes and workflows, rooting them out can be difficult if not impossible to do — even with executive support. For example, in a heavily regulated environment such as stock trading, the use of instant messaging may be subject to retention and auditability rules. IT's role is to educate the traders on the security risks of instant messaging tools, participate in the development of the acceptable use policy (AUP), and subsequently monitor and enforce its use. In this example, that policy could prevent the traders from using Facebook and MSN chat for instant messaging, but enable an internal chat server instead. Governance and management work best if they are based on a set of smart corporate policies that are developed by the four major stakeholders in the enterprise network landscape: IT, HR, executive management, and the users. Clearly IT has a role to play, but it can't be the strictly defined role that it often plays. Neither can IT be lax about its role as the enabler and governor of applications and technology.

APPLICATION CONTROLS

Enablement is about knowing and understanding users and their behaviors, and applications and their associated risks. In the case of popular applications (such as social media), the users have long since decided on the benefits — and are, far too often, oblivious to the threats and risks. As a result, it's vital to match users' needs with the most appropriate applications and features, while also educating users about the implicit risks of those applications and features.

Enabling Facebook usage while protecting the business

Facebook is rapidly extending its influence from the personal world to the corporate world, since employees now use these applications to get their jobs done. At the same time, many organizations are looking at the nearly 1.1 billion Facebook users as an opportunity to conduct research, execute targeted marketing, gather product feedback, and increase awareness. The end result is that Facebook can help organizations improve their bottom line. However, formally enabling the use of Facebook introduces several challenges to organizations. Many organizations are unaware of how heavily Facebook is being used, or for what purpose. In most cases, policies governing specific usage are nonexistent or unenforceable. Finally, users tend to be too trusting, operating in a "click now, think later" mentality that introduces significant security risks. Like any application that is brought into the enterprise by end-users, blindly allowing Facebook usage may result in propagation of threats, loss of data, and damage to the corporate reputation. Blindly blocking Facebook usage is also an inappropriate response because it may play an important role in the business and may force users to find alternative means of accessing it (such as proxies, circumvention tools, and others). Organizations should follow a systematic process to develop, enable, and enforce appropriate Facebook usage policies while simultaneously protecting network resources.

1. Find out who's using Facebook. There are many cases in which a "corporate" Facebook presence may already be established by marketing or sales, so it is critical that IT determine which social networking applications are in use, who is using them, and the associated business objectives. By meeting with the business groups and discussing the common company goals, IT can use this step to move away from the image of "always saying no" and towards the role of business enabler.

2. Develop a corporate Facebook policy. Once Facebook usage patterns are determined, organizations should engage in discussions regarding what should and should not be said or posted about the company, the competition, and the appropriate language. Educating users on the security risks associated with Facebook is another important element to consider when encouraging usage for business purposes. With a "click first, think later" mentality, Facebookusers tend to place too much trust in their network of friends, potentially introducing malware while placing personal and corporate data at risk.

3. Use technology to monitor and enforce policy. The outcome of each of these policy discussions should be documented with an explanation of how IT will apply security policies to safely and securely enable use of Facebook within enterprise environments. As Facebook moves to SSL encryption, enterprises should strongly consider decrypting traffic to and from Facebook. Documenting and enforcing a social networking usage policy can help organizations improve their bottom line while boosting employee morale. An added benefit is that it can help bridge the chasm that commonly exists between the IT department and business groups.

Application enablement typically includes restricting the use of unneeded high-risk applications while managing allowed applications to reduce the inherent risks they may bring with them. Establishing effective policies requires open dialogue among users, IT, and management to truly understand which applications have legitimate business uses and value. Certain applications are known to be conduits for malware, both in terms of infection and ongoing command

and control. Peer-topeer applications, such as BitTorrent, are iconic examples. On the other hand, many applications are not definitively good or bad (black or white), and will instead land in a gray area of enterprise security policy. These applications may have business value but can also carry considerable risk. Safe enablement should be the goal for these applications. In this case, applications can be allowed but constrained to only allow needed features while blocking higher risk features. For example, an enterprise may enable a web meeting application, but not allow the remote desktop capability that could allow a remote attacker to take control of a machine. Enabling policies could also limit certain applications or features to specific approved users, or could scan the application to ensure that no unapproved files or content is being transferred. The ultimate goal is to attack the risk in the application, not the application itself.

Application controls should be part of the overarching corporate security policy. As part of the process of implementing an application control policy, IT should make a concerted effort to learn about new and evolving Web 2.0 applications. This includes embracing them for all their intended purposes and, if needed, proactively installing them or enabling them in a lab environment to see how they act. Peer discussions, message boards, blogs, and developer communities are also valuable sources of information.

USER CONTROLS

Most companies have some type of application usage policy, outlining which applications are allowed and which are prohibited. Every employee is expected to understand the contents of this application usage policy and the ramifications of not complying with it, but there are a number of unanswered questions, including:

✓ Given the ever-growing numbers and types of applications, how will an employee know which applications are allowed and which are prohibited?

✓ How is the list of unapproved applications updated, and who ensures employees know the list has changed?

✓ What constitutes a policy violation? ✓ What are the ramifications of policy violations — a reprimand or termination of employment?

The development of policy guidelines is often a challenging and polarizing process. Determining what should be allowed and what should be prohibited while balancing risk and reward elicits strong opinions from all the major stakeholders. Further complicating the process is the fact that new applications and technologies are often adopted within an organization long before appropriate policies governing their safe and appropriate use are ever considered or developed. Documented employee policies need to be a key piece of the application control puzzle, but employee controls as a stand-alone mechanism will remain largely ineffective for safe enablement of new and evolving applications.

NETWORK CONTROLS

Given that advanced threats most often use the network for infection and ongoing command and control, the network is an obvious and critical policy-enforcement point. With application-enablement policies in place, IT can shift its attention to inspecting the content of allowed traffic. This inspection often includes looking at traffic for known malware, command-and-control patterns, exploits, dangerous URLs, and dangerous or risky file types. When possible, policies that focus on the content of traffic should be coordinated as part of a single unified policy, where the rules (and the results of those rules) can all be seen in context. If content policies are spread across multiple solutions, modules, or monitors, piecing together a coordinated logical enforcement policy becomes increasingly difficult for IT security staff. Understanding whether these policies are working once they are implemented will likewise be difficult. The goal should be to create written policies that reflect the policies' intentions just like someone might describe them orally. For example, "only allow designated employees to use SharePoint, inspect all SharePoint traffic for exploits and malware, disallow the transfer of files types X, Y, and Z, and look for the word confidential in traffic going to untrusted zones." Another key component of network policies is the absolute need to retain visibility into the traffic content. SSL is increasingly used to secure traffic destined for the Internet. Although this may provide privacy for that particular session, if IT lacks the ability to look inside the SSL tunnel,

SSL can also provide an opaque tunnel within which malware can be introduced into the network environment. IT must balance the need to look within SSL against both privacy requirements for end-users and the overall performance requirements of the network. For this reason, it is important to establish SSL decryption policies that can be enforced selectively by application and URL category. For example, social media traffic could be decrypted and inspected for malware, while traffic to financial or healthcare sites is left encrypted.

ENDPOINT CONTROLS

The end-user's machine is the most common target for advanced malware and is a critical point for policy enforcement. Endpoint policies must incorporate ways of ensuring that antivirus and various host-based security solutions are properly installed and up to date. Although targeted attacks are becoming more common, the majority of threats today continue to be known threats with known signatures. Gartner, Inc. predicts that known threats will comprise 95 percent of all threats through 2015. As such, these endpoint solutions must be kept up to date and must be audited regularly. Similarly, you need to have a method for validating that host operating systems are patched and up to date. Many malware infections begin with a remote exploit that targets a known vulnerability in the operating system or application. Thus, keeping these components up to date is a critical aspect of reducing the attack surface of the enterprise. As with employee policies, desktop controls are a key piece to the safe enablement of applications in the enterprise. Desktop controls present IT departments with significant challenges. Careful consideration should be applied to the granularity of the desktop controls and the impact on employee productivity. The drastic step of desktop lockdown to keep users from installing their own applications is a task that is easier said than done and, if used alone, will be ineffective. Here's why:

✓ Remotely connected laptops, Internet downloads, USB drives, and e-mail are all means of installing applications that may or may not be allowed on the network.

✓ Completely removing administrative rights is difficult to implement and, in some cases, severely limits end-user capabilities to an unacceptable level.

✓ USB drives are now capable of running applications, so a Web 2.0 application, for example, can be accessed after network admission is granted.

Desktop controls can complement documented employee policies as a means to safely enable Web 2.0 applications.

ADDRESSING MOBILE AND REMOTE USERS

That the modern enterprise has and continues to become far more distributed than in the past is no secret. Users simply expect to be able to connect and work from any location, whether at an airport, a coffee shop, a hotel room, or at home. This change means that more and more workers and data may be beyond the physical perimeter of the enterprise, and thus also beyond the protections of traditional perimeter security solutions. The key is to build a security architecture that doesn't treat these mobile or remote users as exceptions; they need the same application, user, and content protections when they are outside the perimeter that they would receive when they are inside. Building consistency into the architecture of the network requires careful planning and is a must for any security policy to address the realities of modern computing. Similarly, security policies must address the use of endpoint devices other than standard corporate-issued equipment. Users working from home may use their own personal computers, which are increasingly as likely to be running Apple OSX as they are to be running Windows. Other devices used to remotely connect to enterprise networks include smartphones, tablets, and iOS devices, such as iPhones and iPads. All of these devices must also be addressed in order to prevent blind spots in your organization's security policies. Mobile malware is still in its infancy, but it does exist and is likely to become a major threat in the near future. As mobile devices grow more powerful, they will increasingly be used as a replacement for the PC, storing vast amounts of personal — and valuable — data that is largely unprotected.

CHAPTER SIX 6

TEN BEST PRACTICES FOR CONTROLLING APTS

In This Chapter

▶ Combating malware and APTs with security best practices

In this chapter, I recommend ten best practices to control advanced attacks and APTs. These recommendations are not intended to replace, but rather to supplement, the existing security strategies of your organization, as part of a modern coordinated approach to defense in depth.

ENSURE VISIBILITY INTO ALL TRAFFIC

You can't control what you can't see. Advanced threats are specifically designed to evade legacy port-based firewalls that allow or block traffic based on known TCP and UDP ports. Ensure visibility into all traffic on the enterprise network by:

✓ Accurately classifying all traffic.

- Legacy port-based firewalls that simply match common TCP and UDP ports to a standard protocol are easily bypassed by malware and evasive applications.

- A next-generation firewall uses protocol decoders to fully analyze the application layer and to accurately classify the application and traffic.

✓ Extending visibility beyond the perimeter.

- **Segment the network internally**. Protect high-value targets such as domain controllers and e-mail and database servers, with logical network segmentation (when practical) and special security policies that identify suspicious activity (such as excessive nmap lookups and database queries).

• **Protect remote users**. Deliver the same level of application control, threat prevention, and policy enforcement for remote users and mobile devices outside the network perimeter as for those inside.

RESTRICT HIGH-RISK APPLICATIONS

The number and diversity of applications in the enterprise has exploded, and almost all of them can introduce some level of risk. Although some of these applications may have legitimate use cases, their presence within an enterprise network can introduce a great deal of unnecessary risk into the network. Most applications are designed for easy use, easy sharing, and easy interaction. Security is almost always an afterthought, and it is up to IT security teams to control these risks. Consumerization occurs as users increasingly find personal technology and applications that are more powerful or capable, more convenient, less expensive, quicker to install, and easier to use than corporate IT solutions. According to Gartner, Inc., consumerization will be the most significant trend affecting IT through 2015. Organizations should control the risk introduced by applications by restricting the use of high-risk applications. Here's how:

✓ Block (or limit) P2P applications

✓ Block unneeded applications that can tunnel other applications

✓ Block applications known to be used by malware

✓ Block anonymizers (such as Tor)

✓ Block encrypted tunnel applications (such as UltraSurf)

✓ Limit use of approved proxies to authorized users with a legitimate business need.

✓ Limit use of remote desktop protocols and applications to authorized users with a legitimate business need (such as IT support personnel)

SELECTIVELY DECRYPT AND INSPECT SSL TRAFFIC

Recent analysis of live enterprise networks shows that the reach of SSL is exploding, with roughly 20 to 30 percent of total enterprise bandwidth being consumed by applications that can run SSL (see Figure 6-1).

While SSL certainly provides security for the individual session, it can also create a problem for enterprise security by obscuring the traffic from network security solutions such as intrusion prevention systems (IPS), anti-malware, and data loss prevention (DLP) solutions. To make matters worse, thevery sites and applications that are adopting SSL are the same ones that hackers favor for launching and maintaining their ongoing attacks. IT and security teams should implement best practices and policies to selectively identify, decrypt, and inspect high-risk SSL traffic while maintaining an appropriate balance of performance. Enterprises need to control SSL traffic with:

✓ Decrypt policies that allow decryption and inspection of the following SSL traffic:

    • Social networking • Web-based e-mail

    • Instant messaging • Message boards

    • Microblogging

    • Gaming sites

✓ Do-not-decrypt policies that protect the confidentiality and integrity of the following SSL traffic:

- Health care applications, information, and sites

- Financial applications, data, and sites

- Secure channels

SANDBOX UNKNOWN FILES

Advanced attackers are increasingly turning to customized malware and zero-day exploits targeted at a particular enterprise network or a specific host. This strategy makes the threats extremely unique and almost certainly enables them to pass through security measures without triggering known signatures. This trend highlights one of the limitations in traditional anti-malware security that has existed for years: Signatures can only protect against threats that have been previously detected and analyzed. This reactive approach creates a window of opportunity for cybercriminals (the time that new malware and exploits are "in the wild") in which enterprises are not protected and vulnerable to attack. To address this vulnerability, enterprises should supplement their signature-based tools with direct analysis of unknown files for malicious behaviors. Active analysis is typicallydone by placing the unknown file in a virtual environment to observe how it would behave in a vulnerable environment. This approach can expose some of the tell-tale signs of advanced threats — such as altering operating system files, making changes to registry settings, or injecting themselves into other running processes — and provides IT security teams with a method for definitively identifying malware even when it is not recognized by signature-based anti-malware solutions. IT security teams should have the ability to create protections on demand when new malware or exploits are identified, and distribute these custom protections to all of the organization's network gateways in order to protect against unknown threats. It's not enough to simply put a sandbox into your lab. You must build in the ability to quickly and centrally determine whether a given file has already been analyzed, and then quickly deliver protections to all ingress/egress points when a malicious file is detected.

BLOCK URLS THAT ARE KNOWN TO HOST MALWARE AND EXPLOITS

Even completely valid websites can be compromised and serve up malware or exploits to unsuspecting visitors. However, some sites are clearly more dangerous than others, and a strong URL filtering solution should be able to keep track of sites that have been known to deliver threats. This approach, much like anti-malware and intrusion prevention signature-based solutions, requires constant diligence by the security vendor to keep updated. IT security teams need to challenge their vendors to ensure that URL lists are properly maintained and automatically updated. In addition to known bad sites and URLs, extra caution should be exercised with any recently registered or unclassified domains. Attackers and their threats move quickly between such new sites in order to avoid detection and to cover their tracks. IT security teams must be able to update URL classifications based on malware and exploits that may have been identified through sandboxing. An important benefit of a sandbox is the ability to see how and where the threat came from — andwhere it connects back to. This will allow security teams to immediately update the lists of dangerous URLs, based on actual threats observed in the network.

ENFORCE DRIVE-BY-DOWNLOAD PROTECTION

Infection via drive-by-downloads has become a very common method for malware and exploit delivery. A drive-by-download occurs when a user unknowingly visits a malicious or compromised website that automatically downloads software to the user's computer without the person's knowledge or permission. The host browser and operating system fails to detect or report the download and installation, leaving the user's machine vulnerable to infection. Enterprises must enforce drive-by-download protection to prevent infections by:

✓ Detecting downloads in the background, even unknown exploits and malware

✓ Automatically reporting drive-by-downloads to the user and either blocking the download or requiring the user to acknowledge and permit the download

✓ Training users not to just click "OK" or "Accept" but to read and understand pop-up warnings from their network firewall.

BLOCK KNOWN EXPLOITS AND MALWARE

Although this may seem obvious, known threats (as opposed to new and evolving unknown threats or threats "in the wild") still constitute the majority of threats leading to successful malware infections and attacks against the enterprise today. Malware and exploit kits are increasingly popular and have supercharged the malware economy.

Gartner, Inc., estimates that through 2015, more than 95 percent of malware and exploits will continue to be known threats.

IT organizations commonly disable many known vulnerability signatures and features (such as real-time vulnerability scanning) in intrusion prevention systems or anti-malware software for performance reasons. The single unified threat engine in a true next-generation firewall is designed to process high volumes of network traffic in real-time to detect all threats, without sacrificing performance or reliability.

LIMIT TRAFFIC FOR COMMON APPLICATIONS TO DEFAULT PORTS

Certain ports practically have to be open on a firewall for an enterprise network to function. For example, most web browsing requires TCP ports 53 (DNS), 80 (HTTP), and 443 (HTTPS), and e-mail communication requires TCP port 25 (SMTP). Attackers take advantage of this requirement with malware that regularly communicates on ports that are almost always open by default. Legacy port-based firewalls simply allow traffic across an open port and assume that it is the default application or protocol for that port. A next-generation firewall compares the traffic to application signatures in order to accurately identify the application or protocol, and allows you to set policies that permit only the default application on a common port and block everything else.

EVALUATE NETWORK AND APPLICATION EVENTS IN CONTEXT

It is important to understand that application signatures, network behaviors, and malware sources are all interrelated, and need to be correlated and evaluated in context. Traditional security infrastructures that provide "defense indepth" through separate devices such as port-based firewalls, intrusion prevention, web-content filtering, and anti-malware software can overwhelm security teams with data that cannot be easily correlated.

A true solution should help you make intelligent security decisions based on context, rather than just hoping for a "silver bullet" against a specific threat. To evaluate events in context:

✓ Develop context-based visibility with accurate information about applications, signatures, sources, and behaviors

✓ Correlate events by user and application, including

- Known malware

- Known exploits

- Phone-home detection

- Download history

- URL categories

INVESTIGATE UNKNOWNS

A true next-generation firewall accurately classifies all known traffic and allows you to create customized classifications for any remaining unknowns, such as internal or customdeveloped applications. Unknown traffic should be tracked and investigated to find potential malware or other unidentified threats on the enterprise network. In addition to unknown traffic, you should investigate

✓ **Unknown or unclassified URLs.** Unknown or recently registered URLs are significant because malware and bot-herders regularly rotate between URLs that are used for command and control to impede discovery and takedown efforts. Unknown traffic going to unknown URL categories should be treated as highly suspicious.

✓ **Unknown encryption**. Customized encryption is often used by malware to hide their communications. Use the capabilities of a true next-generation firewall to inspect encrypted traffic and to ensure that all traffic on the network has a known, legitimate purpose.

CONCLUSION

In conclusion, as we navigate the vast digital landscape that resembles the Wild West, it is crucial to acknowledge the potential risks that come with living in an increasingly connected world. The digital realm presents numerous hazards to our privacy, security, and identities, much like the explorers of old who faced unknown dangers in uncharted territories.

Threats including malware, social engineering, cyberstalking, phishing schemes, and many types of fraud abound in the digital world. Even while there is no denying the advantages of our interconnectedness, it is crucial to be aware of the hazards and adopt the appropriate safety measures to guard against harm.

The emergence of advanced persistent threats (APTs) has revolutionized the landscape of network and organizational security. Cybercriminals behind these threats possess unprecedented levels of intelligence, resilience, and patience, making it challenging for conventional security measures to detect and prevent their attacks. Addressing these advanced threats requires collaboration among multiple security disciplines.

Next-generation security solutions offer enhanced visibility, control, and seamless integration of various threat-prevention disciplines. These advancements empower organizations to identify and counter both known and undiscovered attacks effectively. By embracing these cutting-edge approaches, we can better safeguard our digital lives and mitigate the evolving risks that the digital Wild West presents.

In this ever-evolving digital frontier, staying vigilant, informed, and equipped with the latest security measures is crucial to maintaining our privacy, security, and online well-being. By acknowledging the risks and utilizing advanced security practices, we can navigate the digital world with confidence, just as the pioneers of the Wild West forged new paths with resilience and preparedness.